KV-194-977

ENDLESS PATH

Dreamtime

This is a **FLAME TREE** book
First published in 2007

Publisher and Creative Director: Nick Wells
Editor: Cat Emslie
Designer: Lucy Robins
Art Director Mike Spender
Picture Research: Gemma Walters and Toria Lyle
Production: Chris Herbert and Claire Walker

FLAME TREE PUBLISHING
Crabtree Hall, Crabtree Lane
Fulham, London SW6 6TY
United Kingdom
www.flametreepublishing.com

07 09 11 10 08
1 3 5 7 9 10 8 6 4 2

Flame Tree is part of The Foundry Creative Media Company Limited
Copyright © The Foundry 2007

All rights reserved. No part of this publication may be reproduced, stored in a retrieval
system or transmitted in any form or by any means, electronic, mechanical,
photocopying, recording or otherwise, without the prior permission of the publisher.

A copy of the CIP data for this book is available from the British Library.

ISBN 978 1 84451 974 3

Every effort has been made to contact copyright holders. In the event of an oversight
the publishers would be glad to rectify any omissions in future editions of this book.

Printed in China

ENDLESS PATH

Dreamtime

Author: Rachel Storm   Consultant: Dr Nicholas Vlahogiannis

**FLAME TREE
PUBLISHING**

Contents

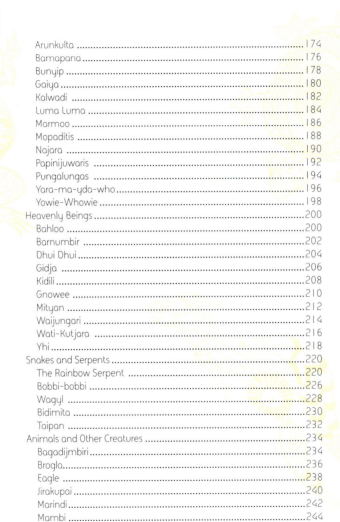

Foreword

For centuries before Europeans actually discovered and settled Australia, they believed that a great southern land, the 'Antipodes' or 'Terra Australis', balanced the land masses of the northern hemisphere.

According to archaeological evidence, the first ancestors of modern Aborigines began arriving on the continent of Australia from Asia some 45,000 years ago. Over the next 20,000–30,000 years, the Aborigines explored and marked out territorial divisions across the continent. By 1788 when the British invaded Australia, the estimated population of Aboriginal people numbered between 300,000 to three million. Australia's Aborigines had formed into approximately 500–600 territorial kingdoms, each with their own family and tribal groups, speaking over 250 different languages and hundreds more dialects. Sophisticated laws governed 'kinship' relationships with their clan families and non-clan members, as well as socio-legal laws and politics.

There is no single Aboriginal way of life, largely because of Australia's size and very diverse environments. Over thousands of years, Aborigines adapted their lifestyles and practices to suit and manage the environment of their territorial lands (such as the selective burning of undergrowth in forests and dead grass on the plains) which stretched for hundreds of kilometres. Here they lived a semi-nomadic lifestyle, travelling around their land according to their six seasons, hunting animals and birds, fishing creeks, rivers and the sea, collecting plants and farming seeds suitable to the terrain. 'Going walkabout', for too long misunderstood by non-Aboriginal people as meaningless wandering, was a complex and organized annual expedition that maintained long established patterns of economic, religious and social contact between the widely separated groups. They invented a wide variety and styles of weapons (boomerangs, clubs and spears) and tools (digging-sticks, axes) made from stone, wood and bone, watercraft such as bark and dugout canoes, domestic implements such as twined-fibre game and fishing nets, and technologies such as permanent stone weir traps. Furthermore, extensive trading networks criss-crossed the continent allowing commodities such as shells, stone, food and finished products such as weapons and tools to be carried and bartered along these trading routes. One much prized commodity was red and yellow ochre, which was very important in Aboriginal artistic and religious life. Ochre mined by the Dieri people of the Lake Eyre Basin in Central Australia was exchanged for a powerful drug called pituri from the peoples of the Simpson Desert 400 kilometres away. Similarly highly valued bailer shells from Cape York Peninsula were exchanged for goods such as boomerangs, shields and ochre across most of Western Australia, Southern Australia and the northern half of Queensland.

The core of Aboriginal life is 'Dreamtime', or an individual's 'Dreaming', a rich body of mythology which explains the world, past and present, to the Aborigine. Dreaming merges with Dreamtime and together encompasses the Aboriginal cosmogony and history, maps out the physical and metaphysical landscapes of every aspect of the land and nature, and serves as a system of beliefs, controlling religious beliefs, rituals and social behaviour and customs. It intimately and inseparably links every Aborigine to their 'country' or territory which, although localized in their perception and representation, is their very essence. It has been, and continues to be, recorded and passed down through countless generations through storytelling and song, religious ceremonies and dances such as corroborees, and the world's longest tradition of artistic expression, bark painting from Arnhem Land, wood-carving and silk-screening from the Tiwi Islands and rock carving and painting from central and western Australia. The wealth of Dreaming is seen in its vast and various subject matters, its very diversity of telling and the fact that Dreaming is not one story or one absolute version, but a plethora of interwoven tellings of the Aborigine's past and present, and their link to their country.

Dr Nicholas Vlahogiannis, University of Melbourne

The Story of Dreamtime

The Arrival of the Aborigines

More than 45,000 years ago the very first explorers entered mainland Australia, most probably from somewhere in Asia, via Indonesian islands through New Guinea. Quite how they made their journey is uncertain. They could have arrived in boats, perhaps blown off course, or maybe they walked from what is now New Guinea over a long-since submerged land bridge. By about 18,000 BC these people had spread out over the entire continent. For thousands of years they persisted in their way of life and their spirituality became entwined with the vast landscape.

The Landscape

The identity of Australia's original inhabitants is intimately connected to the land. As they spread through the continent, they encountered a place of quite extraordinary contrasts. The interior and most of the west is vast arid desert, the mountains to the southeast can be freezing cold, while a tenth of the continent is covered by tropical rainforest.

Many Paths, One Dreamtime

When Europeans arrived in Australia at the end of the eighteenth century they would have found many people already living there (anything between 300,000 and three million, perhaps even more). These earliest inhabitants spoke more than 200 languages and perhaps 600 dialects and were divided into more than 500 groups. Today, they are known collectively as Aborigines or the Indigenous People of Australia, as well as by more localized names such as Koori (the Aborigines from south-eastern Victoria).

According to the Aborigines' traditional beliefs, their origins lie in the Dreamtime and it is this concept of the Dreamtime that links the many different Aboriginal people and their spiritual paths.

Those who lose dreaming are lost.

Traditional Aboriginal saying

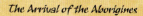

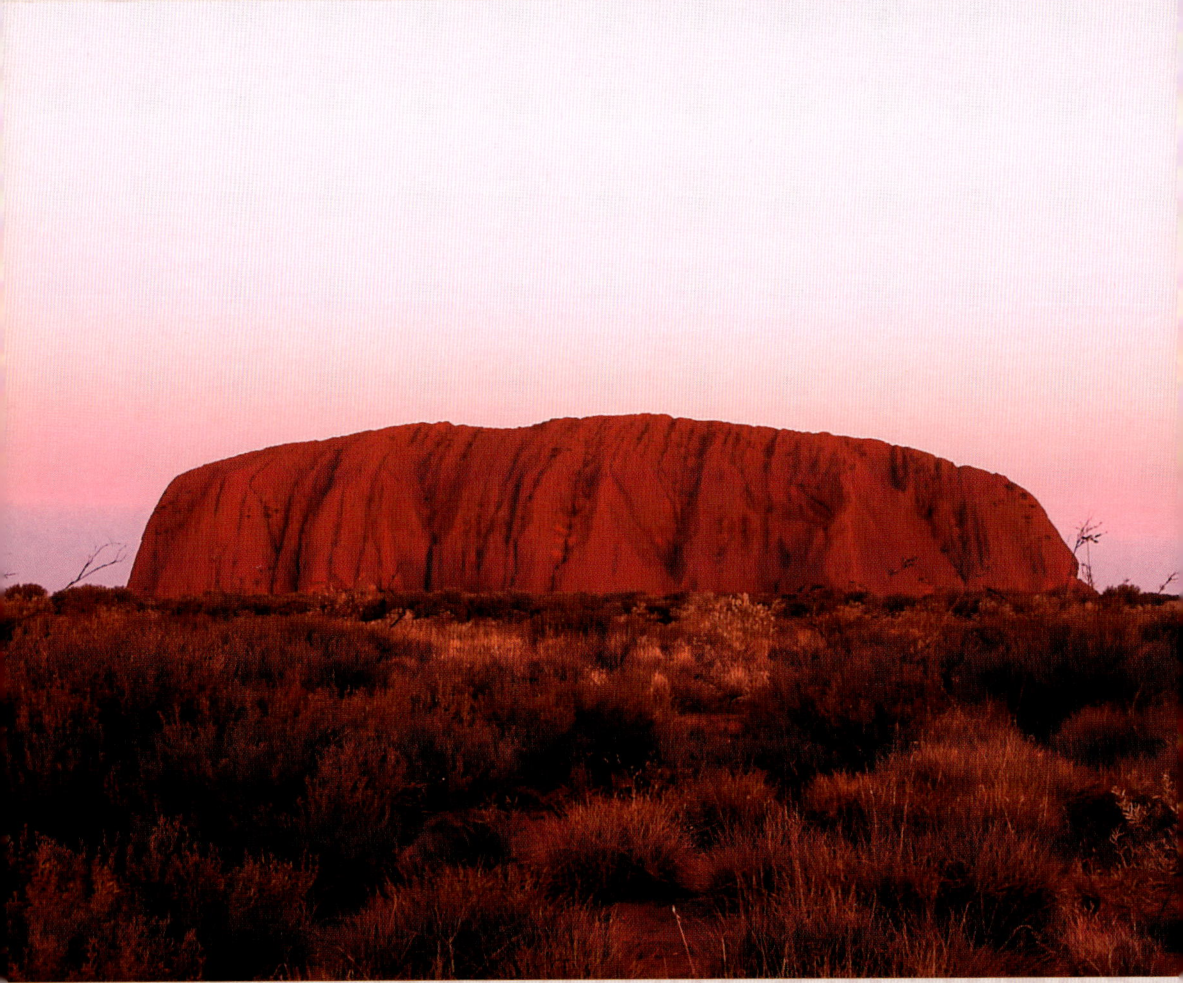

Time and Dreamtime

According to Aboriginal tradition, history begins with the Dreamtime, a period long ago before time began, but which is still with us now. In the Aboriginal world-view time is not linear; there is no word for past or future. Instead, events are often placed in time according to their importance to the individual or community, with important events perceived as being closer to the present.

What Happened in the Dreamtime?

In the Dreamtime, the very first beings emerged from inside the earth, from the sky or from across the seas. Known by many different names, these beings are now often called Ancestors or Ancestral Spirits.

What Did the Ancestors Do?

The Ancestors assumed the forms of humans, animals and superhumans, and moved through the grey, featureless landscape, shaping it with their bodies, creating humans, animals and plants and inspiring a vast network of stories.

Wherever they travelled, the Ancestors left behind them tracks and features, such as rivers, waterholes and hills that can still be seen today. They established relationships between people and animals, instituted laws, and introduced rituals, symbols and languages. Their work completed, they returned to the earth, ascended into the sky or merged with the physical features they had created. They are now asleep, though their spirits are still at work and have the power to affect people's lives.

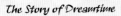

Naming

When the Ancestors first appeared they gave names to the places where they came into existence. Each of these places became a major sacred site. As they travelled through the land, the Ancestors then named all the other places, things and beings; through naming them they brought them into existence.

Songlines

Some say that the Ancestors sang as they made their way across the land; the paths they made are known as songlines, or dreaming tracks.

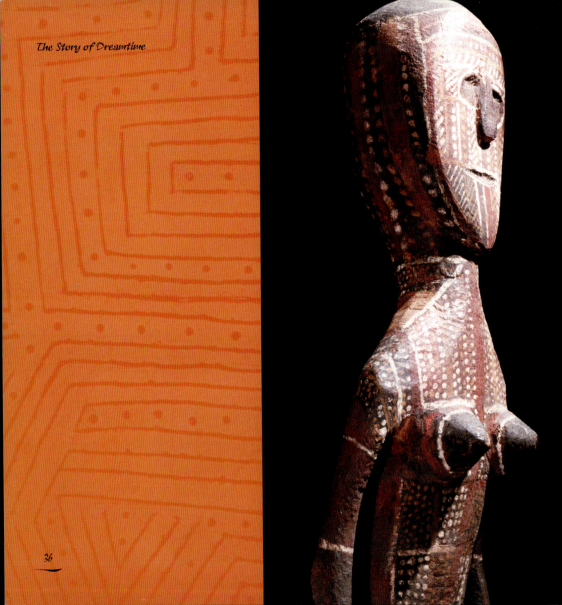

Mother Earth

In many Aboriginal languages the same
word is used for mother, land of the mother
and Ancestor Spirit of the mother's land.

Who Called it Dreamtime?

The term Dreamtime was first used at the very end of the nineteenth century. One report has it that the postmaster of Alice Springs used it as a translation of the Arrernte word *Alcheringa* or *Altyerrenge*; another version is that the famous Australian anthropologist Baldwin Spencer coined the term. There has been much debate over the adequacy of the word, which might also be translated as 'from all eternity'.

Some Aboriginal Words for Dreamtime

Word	People/Language
Altyerrenge	Arrernte
Jukurrpa	Warlpiri
Mura-mura	Dieri
Ngarrangkarni	Gija
Tjukurpa	Pitjantjatjara
Wapar	Yankunytjatjara

The Dreaming

The term 'The Dreaming' is sometimes used interchangeably with Dreamtime to refer to the primordial and eternal time of creation. However, it can also refer to the particular spirituality and beliefs of an individual or group. Everything and everyone has a unique Dreaming, a type of inner understanding of existence, but at the same time all Dreamings overlap, creating a vast web, just as the Ancestors left a network of tracks over the land.

Who Owns the Dreaming?

The events of the Dreamtime are kept alive through the narration, re-enactment and illustration of a vast body of stories. A particular story might belong to an individual or to an entire clan and, through the clan, it will be associated with a particular stretch of land. The story might contain important information, such as the whereabouts of a waterhole and will be carefully passed on to the next generation.

Stories from the Dreamtime are often shared by a number of different Aboriginal groups and are an important source of social cohesion.

Ritual

Two Types

Traditionally, Aborigines use ritual as a way of making direct contact with their Ancestors. There are two main types of ritual. The first, the initiation ritual, often recreates episodes from the Dreamtime through dance, music and a variety of art forms, such as body painting.

Regeneration

The second type of ritual, the fertility or 'increase' ritual, is usually held at a sacred site, for example a rock where an Ancestor rested. There, participants might repaint rock art, scatter blood or perform elaborate dances. The aim is to regenerate the Ancestor's power and also the animal with which it is linked. Adults should ideally perform increase rituals at the site of their totem each year.

Walkabout

The ritual retracing of a path taken by one of the Ancestors is sometimes called a walkabout. The journey is thought to reenergize the powers of the ancient beings and put the traveller in touch with the Dreamtime.

Sacred Energies

Totem

A totem might be an animal, a plant, a rock or a part of the body. Traditionally, each Aborigine is given a totem at birth. Members of the same totemic group are bound to one another and to nature in a special spiritual relationship. Conversely, it may be considered taboo to associate with someone who has an incompatible totem or to kill or eat your own totem. Every totem needs to be nourished by a number of different rituals.

Tjurunga

Many Aborigines say that, as the Dreamtime Ancestors travelled across the land, they carried with them *tjurunga* or *churinga*, sacred objects which they hid in the ground, marking the site with a rock or tree. A *tjurunga* might be a particular stone or a wood carving. Stone *tjurunga* are said to have been made by the Ancestors whereas wood *tjurunga*, carved by the Aborigines, symbolize the *tjurunga* that remain hidden away underground. Each *tjurunga* is believed to hold the essence or spirit of an Ancestor.

A Link with the Dreamtime

Tjurunga are believed to provide a concrete link with the Dreamtime. Each will have particular songs and rituals associated with it and many will be used in secret ceremonies. A young man will only receive his own *tjurunga* after a long and arduous series of tests lasting sometimes more than a decade. When a man dies his spirit is sometimes said to enter the *tjurunga*, which might be buried alongside him.

Guruwari

Some Aboriginal people say that in the Dreamtime, when the Ancestors travelled across the land, they sprinkled *guruwari* or 'seed power' around them as they went. *Guruwari* is seen as the energy of life itself and this same energy exists today, linking the present to the Dreamtime. Everything that happens at a particular place is believed to leave a 'seed' in the earth so that wherever we tread we make contact with all that has happened there.

Medicine Men

Medicine men are believed to have special powers which they can use to heal people, to contact the dead and to discover the cause of unexplained deaths. In some parts of Australia, the Medicine Man's powers are said to come from the Rainbow Serpent. An initiate must go through long periods of meditation and a series of rituals. With his inner eye he can then look inside a person's body and pinpoint his or her ailment. He can also see into the Dreamtime and can rise up to the spirit beings in the sky on a bird or a ray of the sun.

Mabain

Medicine Men are widely believed to gain magical powers through contact with a sacred material called *mabain*. This *mabain* might be contained in a variety of substances including quartz crystals or mother of pearl. It is sometimes inserted into the palms of an initiate's hands or into his tongue. Quartz crystals are considered particularly potent since they refract the light, symbolizing the great ancestral Rainbow Serpent.

Sorcery

Fear of sorcery is still very much a part of Aboriginal life. Sorcerers, sometimes known as *kadaitchas* or *karadjis*, will use their powers to harm suspected murderers and other criminals as well as to punish very minor alleged offenders, for example a woman who has rejected a man's advances. Accusations of sorcery can often follow a death no matter what its cause. The most feared tool of sorcery is the pointing-bone, used to pull someone's life spirit from them.

Rock-art Sorcery

Some secluded rock-art sites show paintings of deformed, horribly twisted men and women, sometimes pierced with long spines and with numerous lumps and swellings. These are sorcery paintings, forming part of a tradition in which artists well versed in magic painted their victims with the afflictions they hoped they would suffer.

At Injalak, a sorcery painting shows a
female figure with twisted intestines,
a broken back, swollen elbows and
knees and a protruding tongue.

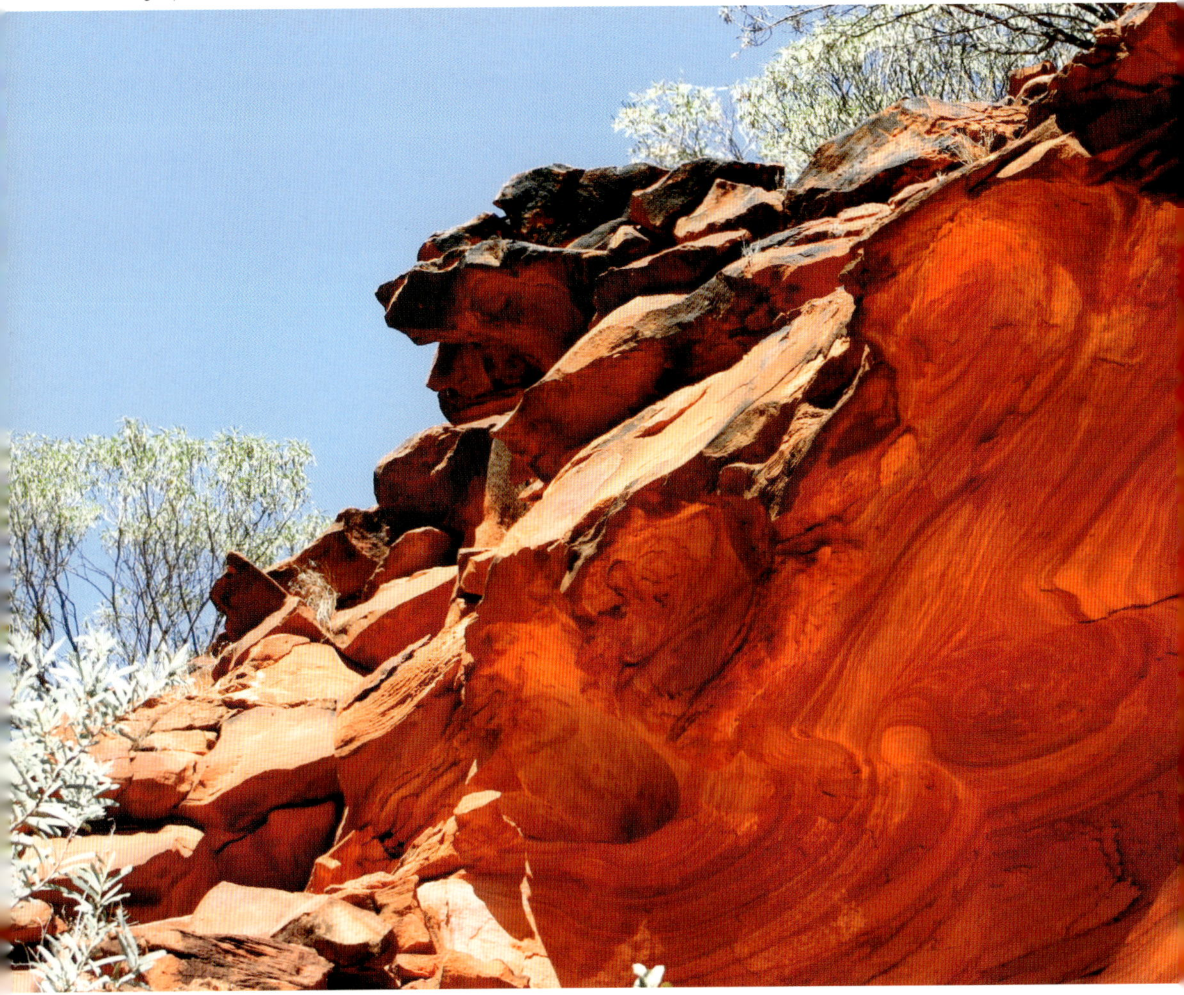

Sources of The Dreaming

Storytelling

The stories and traditions of the Dreamtime have been handed down orally through generations. There is no single orthodox version of a story and not all the stories are available to everyone. Children and non-Aboriginal people will only be told the public level of a story while some stories are open only to initiated males, others only to women. When the Europeans arrived they sometimes banned the telling of traditional stories and many were lost.

Songs

Song can link people to the Dreamtime. It was song which brought the world into existence and it is song which continually recreates it. Traditional songs are usually short and straightforward, often accompanied by clapping sticks, rattles and didjeridus. Particular clans and regions have their own songs; in eastern Arnhem Land the *manikay* song cycle celebrates the Yolngu people's creation stories.

Didjeridu

Traditionally known as the *yidaki* or *gindjunggang*, the didjeridu is a musical instrument made from a log hollowed out by termites or fire and played by blowing into a mouthpiece. Nicknamed the dreampipe, the didjeridu is said to connect listeners to the Dreamtime. Some say that its sound was used to create the world back when the Ancestors moved through the landscape.

Cosmography

The Sky

Traditionally, the Aboriginal universe consists of three planes: the earth, the sky and the underworld. The sky rises above the earth in a dome, sometimes supported at its corners by vast poles. A world of abundant food and water, the sky is home to many Ancestors and is sometimes regarded as the beginning of life, when the spirits of babies fell down from the sky and as the final resting place of mortal souls. The stars in the sky are the campfires of the dead.

The Underworld

The Aboriginal underworld tends to be seen as very similar to the earth, although in some accounts it is dark and inhospitable.

Astronomy

The Aborigines were some of the world's first astronomers.
They named the constellations after the animals
they knew, for example the kangaroo and emu,
and used the stars to tell stories. In particular, the
Kungkarangalpe or Seven Sisters, known to Western
astronomers as the Pleiades, inspired a great many stories,
almost all of which tell how the sisters try to evade
the unwanted advances of a man, sometimes the moon.

Let no one say the past is dead

The past is all about us and within.

Haunted by tribal memories, I know

This little now, this accidental present

Is not the all of me, whose long making

Is so much of the past.

Oodgeroo Noonuccal, 'The Past', from *Inside Black Australia: An Anthology of Aboriginal Poetry*

Life Events

Pregnancy

According to traditional Aboriginal belief, a woman conceives when an Ancestor spirit enters her. The child will often be seen as a descendant of the Ancestor associated with the place where the mother became aware that she was pregnant. Each birth is therefore a link with the past. Sometimes, conception is seen as linked to a particular event, for example a lucky escape from a crocodile. In such a case, the crocodile would be presumed to have conceived the child.

86

Water Spirits

Another tradition holds that the spirits of children live in water. Whenever a man eats fish or turtles it is possible that he will swallow the spirit of a child. Soon afterwards, the man will dream of the child whereupon its spirit will be transferred to the mother and she will become pregnant.

Death

Every living thing is believed to have both a mortal and an immortal soul. The immortal soul is part of an Ancestor and, after death, it will sometimes return to the sacred site of that Ancestor. The mortal soul, on the other hand, fades away.

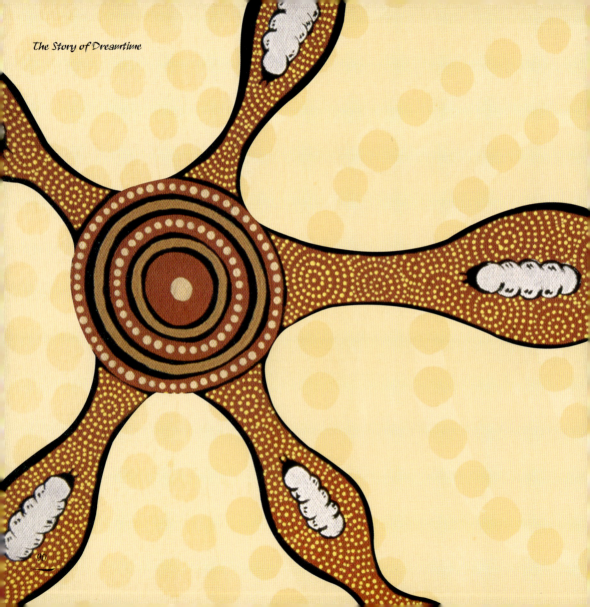

The Story of Dreamtime

90

A Yolngu Tradition

The Yolngu people of Arnhem Land believe that when they die, it is because someone has failed to follow the laws established in the Dreamtime. According to tradition, the dead person is taken in a spirit canoe to an island in the sky known as Baralku. Each night, the campfires of the dead can be seen flickering along the shores of the great Milky Way, called Yiwarra. The canoe returns to earth as a shooting star, reassuring the family of the deceased that he or she has arrived safely in the spirit world.

Contacting the Dead

The Yolngu people gather after sunset to await the rising of the Morning Star. Just before dawn, she appears trailing a rope of light behind her. Using a ritually decorated Morning Star Pole, the Yolngu can then make contact with their deceased friends and family.

Initiation Ceremonies

Male Initiation

Among the Mardudjara Aborigines from the Lake Disappointment region of Western Australia the initiation of boys begins when they are about 11 years old. The child will have a tooth knocked out, his nose will be pierced and he will be circumcised. Afterwards, he will be forbidden to speak for about eight weeks and will be regarded as symbolically dead. He will go on long travels learning about his people's sacred pathways and Dreamings. On his return to everyday society, he will be covered in blood to symbolize his rebirth and will finally be betrothed. However, his full initiation into ritual knowledge will take many more years.

Female Initiation

In traditional Aboriginal society, girls are usually initiated into womanhood as soon as they reach puberty. The ceremonies might include rituals of body-painting and ornamentation, and sometimes scarification.

Art

Rock Art

Aboriginal rock art stretches back possibly 40,000 years, though the date is much disputed. The paintings usually depict humans and animals or consist of highly symbolic designs constructed from circles, zigzags and animal tracks. Made with charcoal and coloured ochres, rock paintings often tell the stories of the Dreamtime Ancestors. The outline of a painting on a rock face might even be seen as the actual imprint of an Ancestor, left when it ended its journey and entered the rock at this particular spot. Some rock-art sites can only be seen by senior Aborigines; others are open to everyone.

The Injalak Ancestor

Many Aborigines say that the image of a human figure at Injalak rock shelter in Arnhem Land must be that of an Ancestor because it is situated too high up the rock face for humans to have created it.

Repainting

The rock paintings at Ubirr in Kakadu National Park depict many different animals, including possums and turtles. Rock-art images of a particular animal were often painted to increase their abundance and to ensure a successful hunt by placing people in touch with the creature's spirit. Some images have been repainted up to modern times. Only people with knowledge of the Dreaming stories are allowed to repaint the images. The process of repainting is regarded as just as important as the final product.

Mimi Art

Some of Australia's very oldest rock art is known as Mimi Art. It can be found in western Arnhem Land in the Northern Territory. The Mimi spirits, described as thin and stick-like, are said to have lived in the land before the Aborigines arrived and to have taught the Aborigines how to paint as well as how to hunt, sing, dance, talk and cook kangaroos. Unlike the Ancestors, the Mimi are not creator beings.

At Ubirr, in Kakadu National Park, a Mimi painting high up on the ceiling of a rock overhang is said by Aborigines to have been created when Mimi spirits squeezed through cracks in the rocks, pulled the ceiling down, painted the image and then pushed the rock back up again.

The X-ray Tradition

The so-called 'X-ray' tradition in Aboriginal art is a style in which animals and humans are depicted with their insides visible: the spinal column, ribs and internal organs can all be seen. The X-ray style was particularly popular at Ubirr in western Arnhem Land, where Aborigines camped during the wet seasons. X-ray paintings are also found at Injalak in Arnhem Land; a community of artists continues to work in the tradition nearby.

Gwion Gwion

In the Kimberley region of North West Australia, the distinctive Gwion Gwion rock-art paintings are believed by some researchers to date back at least 17,000 years. According to tradition, the paintings were made by birds that pecked the rocks until their beaks bled and then painted the images with their tail feathers. In traditional belief, Gwion Gwion is the name of a long-beaked bird that was originally a spirit being who cracked open rocks revealing the stone tools inside. The paintings are sometimes called Bradshaw figures after Joseph Bradshaw who in 1891 was the first European to discover them.

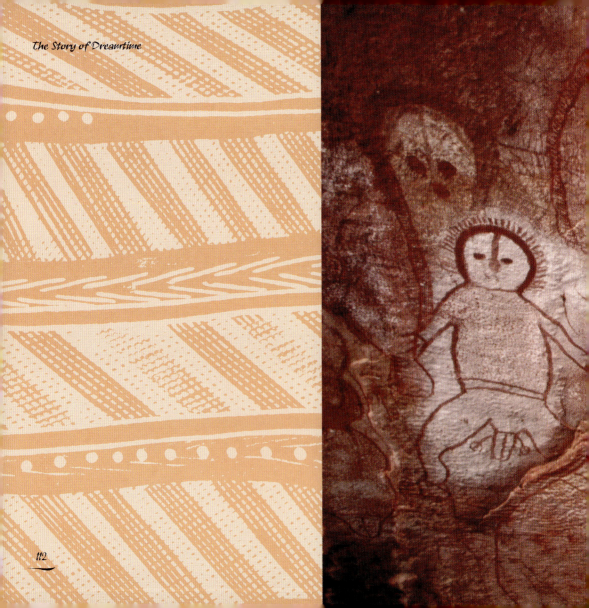

Wondjinas

The rock-art figures known as Wondjinas or Wandjinas are the Ancestors of the Aboriginal people of the Kimberley region. The images sometimes loom as much as 6 m (20 ft) high. They have large white faces and their heads are usually surrounded by something resembling a halo. According to traditional belief, the Wondjinas came out of the sky, created the world and lived on the land. Before departing, they painted their images and then disappeared inside the rocks. The ritual of repainting the images is said to hasten the beginning of the wet season.

The Wondjinas are still very powerful. They will strike anyone who shows them disrespect with lightning or call up floods and great winds.

Aboriginal achievement

Is like the dark side of the moon,

For it is there

But so little is known

Ernie Dingo, from *Inside Black Australia: An Anthology of Aboriginal Poetry*

Bark Paintings

In preparation for the wet season, Aborigines would sometimes build shelters from bark and paint the walls with images that told stories from the Dreamtime. Today, Aboriginal bark paintings have entered the international fine-art market, though the stories behind the paintings are not always made fully available to the buyers for fear of offending the spirits.

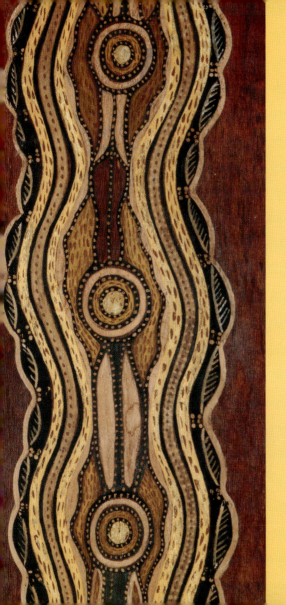

Body Art and Scarification

Body painting carries enormous spiritual significance for Aborigines. Used mostly in funeral ceremonies and initiation rituals, the intricate designs indicate an individual's social and family relationships and enable him or her to become filled with the power of the Dreamtime. Decorated with leaves, feathers and other objects, a participant might even 'become' one of the great Ancestors. Until recent times, scarification was also widely used as a way of indicating an individual's status in society.

Sacred Sites

Dreamtime Landmarks

To the Aborigines' way of thinking, the whole of creation is a sacred site. Within this broad, sacred landscape, particular areas and sites are more revered than others since they bear witness to important events that occurred long ago in the Dreamtime.

Uluru

Uluru or Ayers Rock is situated in the very centre of Australia, in Northern Territory. The deep red monolithic sandstone outcrop, some 10 km (six miles) in diameter, is of immense spiritual significance to the Aborigines and is associated with numerous Dreamtime stories. In some accounts, it is here that the powerful Rainbow Serpent emerged from a giant rainbow.

Kata Tjuta

Like Uluru, Kata Tjuta – or 'The Olgas'– also in Northern Territory, is of great spiritual significance to the Aborigines and plays a prominent role in stories of the Dreamtime. The largest of Kata Tjuta's many red mounds is home to the snake Wanambi. During the rainy season, Wanambi lies curled in a waterhole on the summit, but when it becomes dry he slides down. The dark lines on the east side of the mountain are said to be the hairs of Wanambi's beard and his breath is the wind blowing through the gorge. It is forbidden to light fires in the area or to drink at the waterhole in case Wanambi is angered and launches an attack.

Lake Narran

In New South Wales, several hundred kilometres northwest of Sydney, lies Lake Narran. It was here, thousands of years ago, that the great creator Baiame decided to appear on earth as a mortal. When the time arrived, every living creature gathered by the lake to welcome him. Baiame drew a circle on the ground, representing his body from which all life comes. He then instructed the Aborigines to hold initiation ceremonies and so it was that the tradition of holding initiation ceremonies within a circle was established.

Alice Springs

There is a tradition that in the Dreamtime the sun first came out of the ground at Alice Springs, in the form of a female Ancestor spirit. The site is now marked by a large stone.

131

Beings of the Dreaming and Beyond

Great Creators

Altjira

The great creator being of the Arrernte people of Central Australia, Altjira is said to have made the earth and then retired to the heavens. He still lives in the sky, indifferent to the lives of men and women. Altjira is usually represented as a man with the feet of an emu. The word is sometimes used more generally to refer to the Dreamtime.

Baiame

The great father and creator spirit of many Aborigines of the
High Plains and south-east Australia, Baiame made people
and places and could summon up rain and floods.

Bunjil

According to the Kulin and Wurunjerri people of central Victoria, Bunjil shaped the landscape assisted by six wise men. He then fashioned the first man and woman from bark and clay, named them and breathed life into them through their mouths, nostrils and navels. He also taught mankind the arts of life. His work complete, he retired to the sky.

The Djanggawul

The Djanngawul (or Djanggau) are three siblings, one male and two female. The Yolngu people of Arnhem Land in north Australia say that long ago in the Dreamtime, they lived on an island, 'The Land of the Dead', far out at sea. One day, they decided to come to the mainland. They landed near Port Bradshaw and made their way through the land, creating everything in it and placing sacred objects in the ground. Song cycles and stories of the Djanggawul underlie many of the ceremonies performed by the Yolngu people. One tale tells how the sisters were both male and female until their brother cut off their male parts.

Eingana

All the creatures of the world took shape inside Eingana, a snake goddess, but the great Ancestor had no hole by which to give birth. She grew and grew in size, suffering increasing agonies, until at last another Ancestor pierced a hole in her. Eingana is attached to every living being by a tendon. If she lets go, the creature will die.

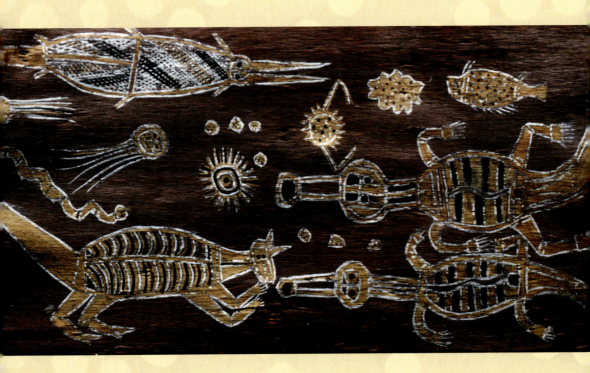

The Ungambikula and the Inapertwa

Long ago, say the Aranda (Arrernte) people of Central Australia, some very rudimentary human beings known as Inapertwa lived beside the sea. These creatures had no limbs, eyes, ears or noses; they were just indistinct mounds. Two great Ancestral Spirits called Ungambikula ('out of nothing') came down from the sky and, wielding their large stone knives, they proceeded to cut these creatures open, turning them into men and women.

Kurriyala

Long ago, say the Kuku-Yalanji people of the North Queensland rainforest, the great Ancestor Spirit, the Rainbow Serpent Kurriyala, appeared from the west. He formed Narabullga (Mount Mulligan), from his droppings and made a huge lake at the top. Next, he made another mountain; this one was in the shape of a snake and he called it Naradunga (Mount Mulgrave). Kurriyala continued shaping the landscape until at last he revealed himself to his people and showed them how to dance and paint their bodies.

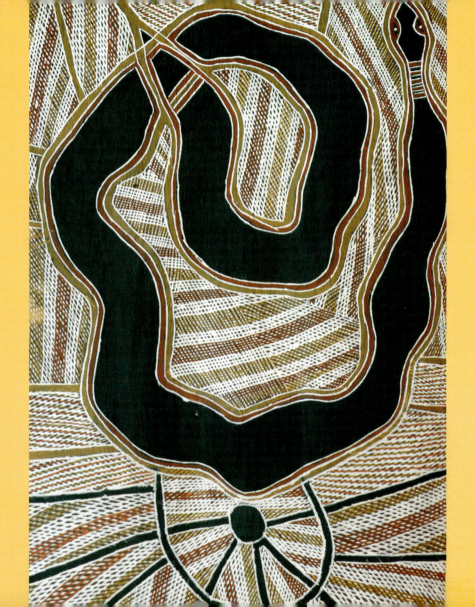

Minawara

According to the Nambutji people of Central Australia there was once a great flood. Afterwards, the kangaroo Ancestor Minawara emerged from the debris together with his brother Multutu. Together, they wandered the earth, shaping the landscape and introducing initiation rites.

Mudungkala

The great Ancestor of the Tiwi people of Melville and Bathurst Islands off the north coast of Australia, Mudungkala (or Mudunungkarla) was an old blind woman who emerged from beneath the ground. She crawled slowly northwards on her knees, carrying her three children with her, and the water that bubbled up behind her formed the Dundas Strait. Next, Mudungkala made the Tiwi islands, filled them with plants and animals and finally crawled away leaving her children behind to enjoy her creation.

Pundjel

According to the traditional teachings of the Aborigines of Southeast Australia, Pundjel made the first human beings, two men, from clay and bark.

They were each given a wife by Pundjel's brother, Pallian. In due course the wives had children but the children were so wicked that Pundjel and Pallian cut them into pieces. It is from these pieces that the Aborigines are descended.

Waramurungundi

According to the Gunwinggu people of Arnhem Land, Waramurungundi was the first woman and the mother of all creation. She gave birth to the earth, fashioned every living creature and crossed the land sowing plants and making waterholes with her digging stick. Afterwards, she taught people how to speak and divided each language group from the next. Her work complete, she turned into a rock.

Yingarna

An important Ancestor Being for the Kuninjku people of Arnhem Land, Yingarna emerged from the sea at Malay Bay wearing a head ring from which hung 15 dillybags (traditional woven bags) full of babies. She dropped the babies off at different places throughout the region and taught them how to speak different languages, how to hunt and how to plant yams. When she had found the ideal home for each of her children, she left. Thus she was responsible for the creation of the Aboriginal people. At one point on her travels, Yingarna gave birth to a son, the Rainbow Serpent Ngalyod.

I am a child of the Dreamtime People

Part of this Land, like the gnarled gumtree ...

... I am this land

And this land is me

I am Australia

'Spiritual Song of the Aborigine', Hyllus Maris,
from *Inside Black Australia: an Anthology of Aboriginal Poetry*

Heroes and Other Humans

Djamar

Long ago in the Dreamtime, the great hero Djamar established many of the rituals known to the Aborigines of Australia's West Kimberley region. Djamar came from the sea and rested for three days before making a huge bullroarer (an ancient instrument) which he swung round and round, felling all the trees in the area. Next, he shattered boulders with his bullroarer, creating fragments of rock which the people made into stone knives. At Djarinjin he was wounded by a rock fish and began to bleed, his blood filling a rock basin. Ever since then, Djamar has been associated with ritual blood-letting.

Djanbun

According to the Aborigines from the Clarence River region of New South Wales, Djanbun was a man who once blew on a fire-stick in an attempt to make it burst into flame. As he blew harder and harder, his mouth grew bigger and bigger until eventually he turned into a platypus and fled into the river.

Erathipa

The word 'Erathipa' means 'child', although it has come to be associated with particular stones. One such stone, near Alice Springs, stands about 1 m (3 ft) high. It is said that, in the Dreamtime, a woman was unable to find her sacred Nurtunja pole and so, placing her baby on the ground, she went in search of it. The baby burrowed into the earth, marking the site with a stone. Still unable to find her pole, the woman fell down dead. Ever since then, spirit children have looked out through a hole in the Erathipa stone, searching for women to mother them. It is traditionally believed that visiting the stone will result in conception.

Ginga

Aborigines from the Kakadu National Park region say that at the very beginning of time, a man called Ginga was sleeping by a fire when his back began to burn. Awaking with a start, Ginga flung himself into a billabong whereupon his skin broke out in large blisters. From that time onwards, Ginga was a crocodile; his mishap explains why, to this day, the crocodile has such lumpy skin. Ginga the crocodile then proceeded to help shape the Kakadu landscape until, his work complete, he turned into a rocky ridge at a place called Djirringbal.

Gulibunjay

The Yarrabah Aborigines of Queensland say that once, long ago, there was a man called Gulibunjay (or Galibunjay) whose son, Wangal, was a boomerang. One day, Gulibunjay threw Wangal far out into the ocean, but the boomerang failed to return. Gulibunjay searched everywhere for his son, naming every living thing as he did so. Sadly, he never found Wangal and to this day he sits on a mountain looking out to sea, still hoping that one day the boy will return.

Kondili

A traditional tale from the Kaurna and Ngarrindjeri people of South Australia tells how, long ago in the Dreamtime, there was a man called Kondili (or Kondole) whose feet made sparks when he walked. Everyone who saw him was utterly amazed since they had never seen fire before. A man called Tiritpa grew jealous and one day decided to steal Kondili's fire. He invited Kondili to a party on a beach and when everyone was enjoying themselves dancing around the huge fire Kondili had made, he and his friend threw their spears at the luckless man. Kondili was in such pain that he jumped into the sea where he turned into a whale, a gush of water spurting from his wound.

Wuragag

The Gunwinggu people of Arnhem Land say that Wuragag was the very first man. He was very lazy and so his wife, Waramurungundi, turned him into stone, along with two of his women friends. The three hills can be seen to this day.

Monsters, Tricksters and Evil Spirits

Arunkulta

In Arrernte tradition, Arunkulta is the spirit of
evil. The great lizard Mangar-kunjer-kunja
protected people from Arunkulta's influence.

Bamapana

According to the Murnging people of northern Australia, Bamapana is a trickster being who causes outrage by breaking taboos, in particular the taboo of tribal incest.

Bunyip

Long ago, there was an Aborigine who ignored his people's rules and ate his own totem animal. Baiame banished him whereupon the man became an evil water spirit called Bunyip. This Bunyip was a bellowing, monstrous creature about the size of a calf. He lived in waterholes and roamed around at night threatening to devour anyone he came across. Some young women once tried to spy on Bunyip, whereupon the monster enslaved them and turned them into water spirits. To this day, the women lure hunters into dark and dangerous waters where they drown.

Gaiya

The people of Mornington Island in the Gulf of Carpentaria say that there was once an old grasshopper woman, Ealgin, who came from the west with a giant dog called Gaiya. Both the dog and the woman hunted humans for food. One day, Gaiya set off in pursuit of two young men, the butcherbird brothers. However, these brothers proved far too clever for the dog and succeeded in killing the massive beast; afterwards, they invited all their people to come and eat him. The brothers sent Gaiya's spirit to the grasshopper woman, but by now the spirit was so angry that it jumped up and bit the grasshopper woman on the nose, leaving marks which can be seen to this day on the noses of all grasshoppers.

Kalwadi

The Murinbata people of the Port Keats region of Northern Australia recall how once, long ago in the Dreamtime, the old woman Kalwadi was looking after her people's children when, fed up with the task, she swallowed ten of them whole. The children's parents returned and, realizing what had happened, they cut Kalwadi open and removed the children. To everyone's relief, they were still alive.

Luma Luma

A giant Ancestral Spirit from the Dreamtime, Luma Luma is said to have arrived in Arnhem Land from across the seas, perhaps from Indonesia or from Macassar. He transformed himself into a stingray so that he could travel through the sea more easily but, once on the mainland, he turned back into a giant. At first, the Gunwinggu people attacked Luma Luma but when they realized he meant them no harm, they lived together peacefully.

Marmoo

According to traditional Aboriginal belief, Marmoo is an evil spirit at war with the great Ancestor Baiame. Jealous of Baiame's power, Marmoo determined to prove himself by creating a swarm of insects. After breathing life into them, he sent them out from his cave as a vast black cloud that left a trail of misery behind it. To help men and women, Baiame created birds so that they might eat the insects. When the birds had done their job, Baiame rewarded them by giving them their beautiful voices.

Mopaditis

According to the Tiwi people of Melville Island, the Mopaditis
are the spirits of the dead. They look like humans but their
bodies lack substance. The Mopaditis cannot be seen by day
but at night they appear white, sometimes walking on the
surface of water.

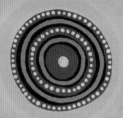

Najara

The Aborigines of Western Australia say that Najara is a wicked spirit whose whistling lures young boys away from their people and persuades them to forget their language and culture.

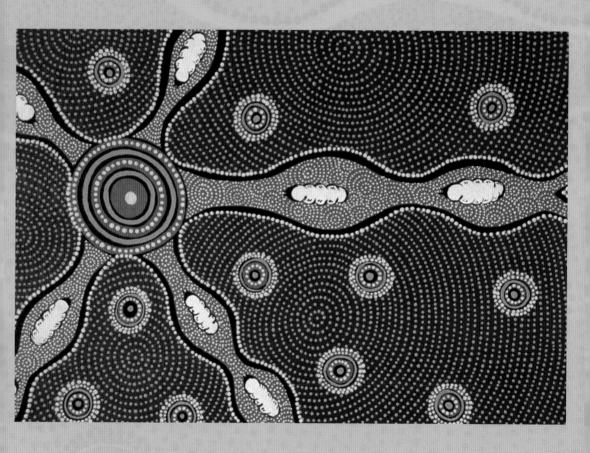

Papinjuwaris

According to the Tiwi people of Melville Island, the Papinjuwaris are one-eyed giants who live in a hut at the end of the sky. They stride through the heavens wielding fire-sticks. From earth, they look like shooting stars. Papinjuwaris suck blood from the sick and climb in through their victims' mouths to drain the last drops.

Pungalungas

Long ago in the Dreamtime, in the region of Uluru in the Northern Territory, there lived a race of giant cannibals called Pungalungas or Pungalunga Men. A fierce battle left only one Pungalunga alive. This solitary Pungalunga came across the mice women who had never set eyes on a man. When the Pungalunga attacked one of the women, the others all fell on him until he ran off.

Yara-ma-yha-who

According to Aboriginal tradition, the Yara-ma-yha-who is a small, red, toothless man with fingers and toes shaped like the suckers of an octopus. He lives in the tops of fig trees and waits for people to shelter underneath, then jumps down, clings onto the person with his suckers and drinks the victim's blood. The Yara-ma-yha-who then swallows his victim but later regurgitates him or her, still alive. If someone is caught and swallowed several times they begin to shrink. This story is told to young children to frighten them from wandering off from camp.

Yowie-Whowie

A cross between a lizard and an ant, the Yowie-Whowie crawls out of the ground at night and eats everything it comes across, including humans.

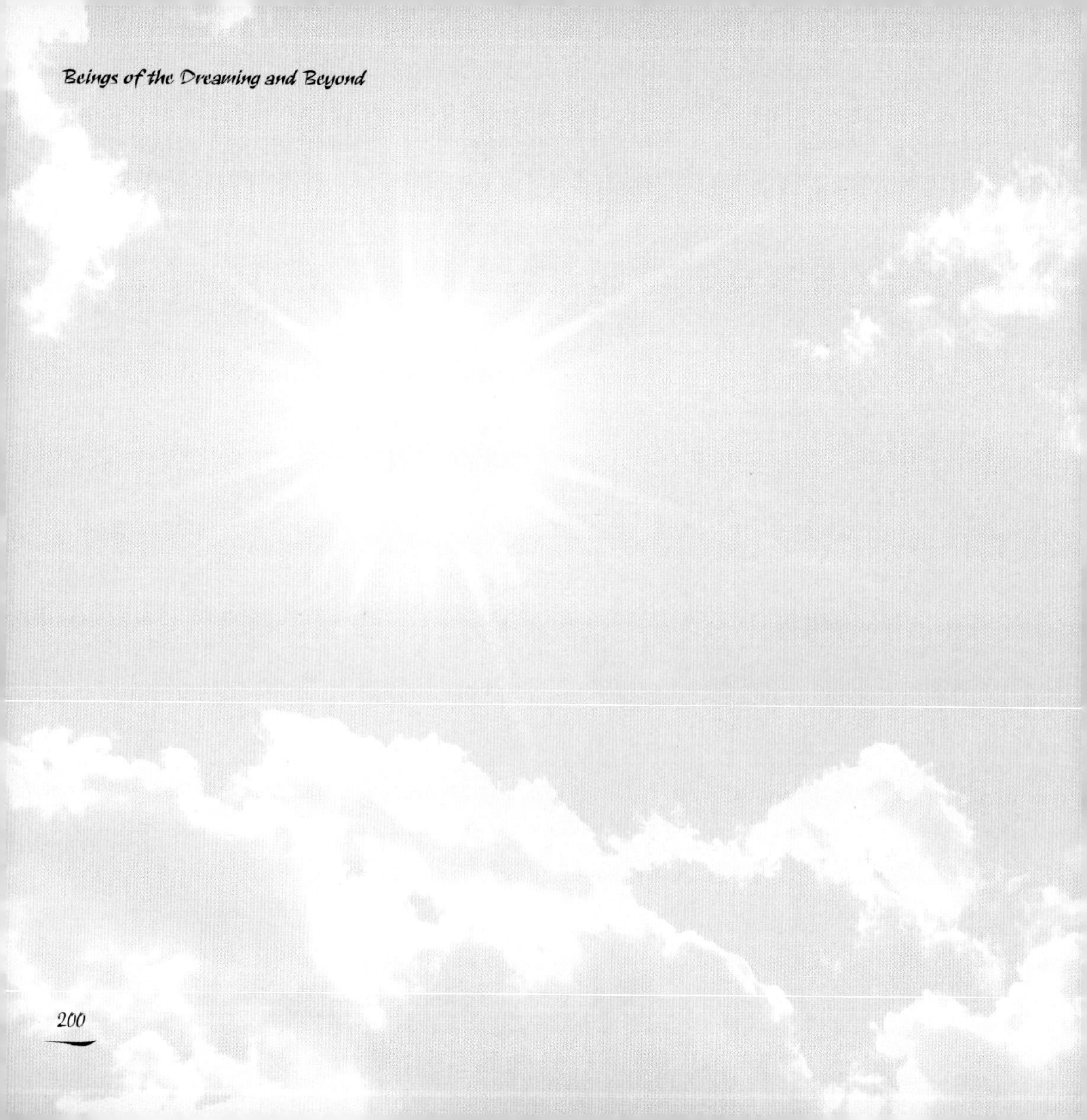

Heavenly Beings

Bahloo

The Aborigines of Central Australia say that there was once a man called Nullandi whom the great Ancestor Baiame looked on very kindly. When Nullandi grew old, Baiame raised him to the sky where he became Bahloo, the moon. Yhi, the sun, made advances towards Bahloo but the moon drew back, afraid of her ardour. To this day, Yhi can be seen chasing Bahloo across the sky.

Barnumbir

A story from Arnhem Land in the north of Australia tells how the girl spirit, Barnumbir, the morning star, lives on Bralgu, the Island of the Dead. When people went fishing they would ask Barnumbir to accompany them in order to light their way. Terrified of drowning, Barnumbir always refused. Eventually, two women tied a long string around Barnumbir so that, should she fall in to the water, they could pull her back to land. However, because she is tied to the string, Barnumbir cannot rise very high in the sky.

Dhui Dhui

The Bandjin people of Hinchinbrook Island and Lucinda Point on the mainland of North Queensland tell a story about two boys called the Dhui Dhui. One day, these boys paddled out in their canoe and began to fish precisely where their elders had told them not to. The Elders were afraid the boys would be attacked by a huge shovelnose ray that lived there. Before long, the ray bit the boys' line and began to tow them around and around. The boys would not let go of the line and eventually they disappeared out of sight beyond the horizon. That night, they appeared in the sky as the constellation known as the Southern Cross.

Gidja

According to the traditions of the Bullanji people of north-east Australia, Gidja is the moon spirit. People laughed at him for being round and fat but he courted the evening star so assiduously that she agreed to marry him. Another story tells how he castrated Yalungur in order to create the first woman.

kidili

The Mandjindja people of Western Australia say that Kidili was a moon man who tried to rape some of the first women. The two brothers known as the Wati-kutjara castrated Kidili with a boomerang and he died of his wounds in a waterhole. The women he attacked became the Kungkarangalpe (the Pleiades).

Gnowee

The Boorong people of Victoria say that Gnowee, the sun, was created when an emu egg was thrown into the sky. Others say that long ago there was a woman called Gnowee who travelled everywhere looking for food for her son until she stepped off the end of the world and became the sun.

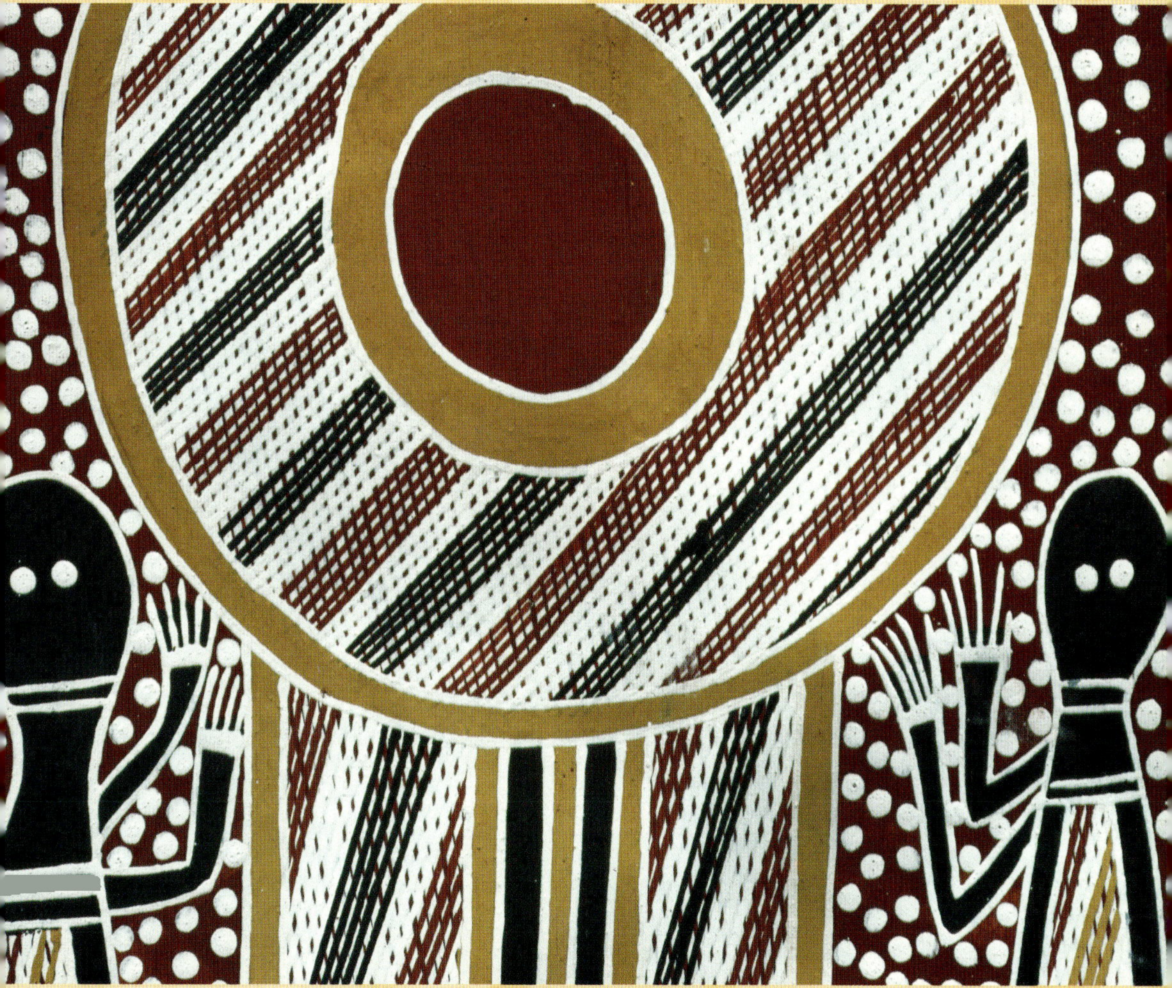

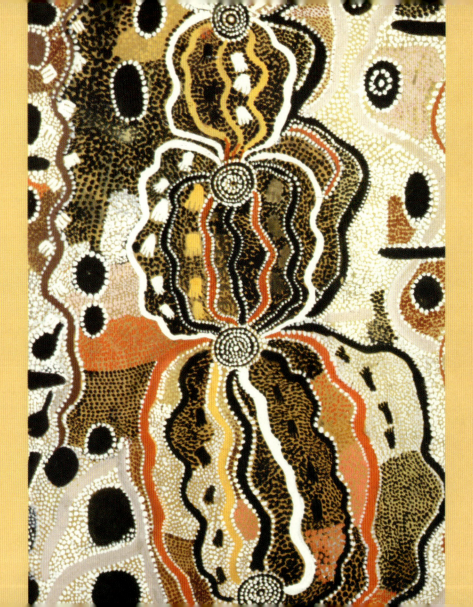

Mityan

Long ago, say the Boorong people of northwest Victoria, there was a native cat (a kind of marsupial with round and crescent-shaped marks on its body) who tried to persuade a man's wife to run away with him. When his plot was discovered, he was severely beaten and ever since then he has been wandering through the skies as the moon.

Waijungari

The Jaralde clan of the Ngarrindjeri people

of South Australia say that the planet Mars is

the man Waijungari who fled into the sky, still

covered in the red ochre of his initiation ritual,

when it was discovered that he had slept with

the two wives of a man called Nepele.

Wati-kutjara

The Aborigines of Central Australia and the Outback say that the Wati-kutjara were lizard men who lived during the Dreamtime. They once saved a group of women who were being chased by the moon man, striking and killing him with their boomerangs. The women became the Kungkarangalpe (Pleiades) and the Wati-kutjara became the constellation Gemini.

Yhi

According to the Aborigines of Central Australia, Yhi is the spirit of the sun, light and creation. She appeared long ago in the Dreamtime and walked through the land bringing plants into being and giving creatures their unique characteristics.

Snakes and Serpents

The Rainbow Serpent

The cult of the Rainbow Serpent is one of the longest unbroken spiritual traditions in the world. The great snake lives in waterholes, presiding over rain and floods and thereby controlling the availability of water. Different groups tell a number of stories about her and she is known by many names including Almudj, Julungul, Galeru, Ungur, Wonungur, Worombi, Yurlunggur, Kalseru, Langal, Ngalyod, Ungud, Wullunqua and Muit.

Almudj

Long ago in the Dreamtime, the Rainbow Serpent Almudj created rock formations and waterholes in the landscape of Kakadu National Park in Australia's Northern Territory. The Gagudju people say she still lives at Djuwarr in a dark pool at the bottom of a waterfall. When she rears up onto her tail, she forms a rainbow.

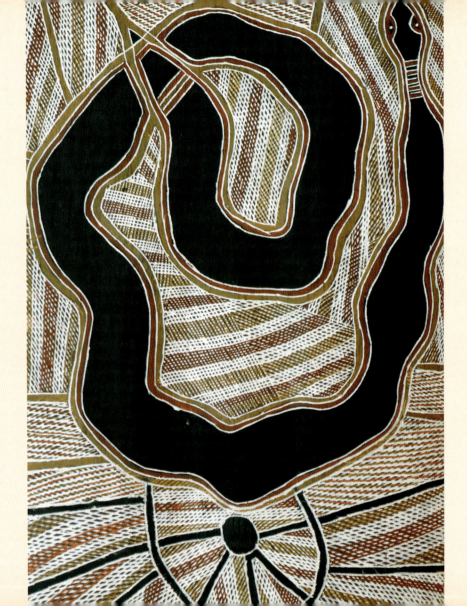

Yurlunggur

The Yolngu people of northeastern Arnhem Land say that Yurlunggur (Julunggul) is a mighty Rainbow Serpent who caused a great flood when one of the Wawilak sisters allowed her blood to flow into Yurlunggur's waterhole. In her fury, Yurlunggur swallowed the sisters but eventually regurgitated them.

Bobbi-bobbi

The great ancestral serpent of the Binbinga people of northern Australia, Bobbi-bobbi fashioned the first boomerang from one of his ribs and gave it to the Binbinga so they could feed themselves by killing flying foxes. One day, the Binbinga knocked a hole in the sky with the boomerang. Infuriated, Bobbi-bobbi seized the weapon, devouring the two men who tried to keep hold of it.

Wagyl

A snake-like creature, sometimes described as a winged serpent, the Wagyl is an important Ancestor of the Nyoongah (Noongar) people of south-west Western Australia. The Wagyl is both male and female, one and many. Ordered by the Rainbow Serpent to look after fresh water sources, he lives in waterholes, rivers and springs and will cause untold harm to anyone who disturbs him.

Bidimita

According to tradition the Bidimita are brightly
coloured serpents more than 15 m (50 ft) long
and with terrifyingly sharp teeth. In the wet season,
they travel over the land in large thunderclouds; their
voices are the thunder and their tongues are the lightning.

Taipan

The brown snake spirit of the Wik Kalkan people of Cape York peninsula in the north of Australia, Taipan controls life and death. He gave humans their blood and is able to alter its flow and supply.

Animals and Other Creatures

Bagadjimbiri

According to the Karadjeri people of north-west Australia, the Bagadjimbiri brothers are great creator beings who emerged from the ground as dingoes. As the sun rose, the two brothers made the first waterholes and began to name the plants and animals. When it was time for them to leave the world, they turned into watersnakes and their spirits rose into the sky as great clouds.

Brolga

A large grey crane found in the lowland floodplains of south-east Australia, Brolga appears in a number of traditional stories. In one tale, Emu pushes Brolga's beak into the ground to make fresh water springs and in another Brolga is wounded in a fight, leaving him with a red mark on his head.

Eagle

Throughout much of Australia the Crow and the Eagle or Eaglehawk serve symbolically to divide Aboriginal communities into two halves or 'moieties'. According to one story, long ago in the Dreamtime, there was a mosquito that became a blowfly, then a small bird and finally a Crow. Finding himself all alone, Crow decided to trick another creature down from a tree. He made a fire, stuck a sharp bone into the ground with its pointed end sticking upwards and sang a song challenging that he would catch any creature that came down from the tree. One creature, an Eaglehawk, jumped and was impaled on the bone.

Crow purified Eaglehawk on his fire and took her to his camp where they became the first Crow man and Eaglehawk woman, the Ancestors of the Aboriginal moieties. From that time onwards everyone had to marry into the opposite moiety.

Jirakupai

The Aborigines of Bathurst Island say that long ago in the Dreamtime a man called Jirakupai lived beside a pool with his wives, the sisters Kuraruna and Jaknia. Jirakupai was a skilled craftsman and made many splendid spears. When he had just completed a number of weapons, some men from Melville Island attacked his camp, spearing him in the back. Jirakupai simply pulled out the spears and hurled them back at his attackers, then dived into the pool. The next morning, the men from Melville Island saw Jirakupai floating in the water. He had turned into a crocodile: the spear wounds in his back had become the crocodile's ridged spine and his bundles of spears had become his tail.

Jirakupai's wives, Kuraruna and Jaknia, became birds. Kuraruna became the night heron and Jaknia became the brown heron.

Marindi

Long ago in the Dreamtime, the lizard Adnoartina, the guardian of Uluru, challenged the dingo Marindi to a fight. The lizard persuaded Marindi to wait until evening when he could see better and then he leapt at Marindi's throat, killing him. The blood stained the rocks red and they have remained that colour to this day.

Mambi

The Adnyamathanha people of the northern Flinders Ranges say that there was once a man who swept some bronze-winged pigeons up in a net and then hit them with his club. Only one, called Mambi, managed to escape. Mambi rose into the air dropping feathers and blood as he flew and leaving more wherever he rested. The feathers and blood turned into gold and quartz and can still be found today.

Wahn

A story from the Aborigines of Victoria, tells how Wahn the Crow stole fire from the seven sisters known as Meamei, who here were custodians of the gift of fire, which they kept hidden in yarn sticks. Discovering that the women were terrified of snakes but fond of termites, Wahn secretly hid some snakes in a termite mound. When the women broke open the mound, the snakes reared up and attacked them whereupon the women waved their fire-sticks around. Some embers fell from the sticks and Wahn quickly made off with them, held between two pieces of bark. After this the sisters became the star cluster Kungkarangalpe (the Pleaides).

Wembulin

A bloodthirsty spider, Wembulin was one of the Ancestors of the Wotjobaluk people of Victoria. He had many adventures as he shaped the landscape.

Yurlu

According to the Adnyamathanha people of the northern Flinders Ranges, Yurlu was the kingfisher who helped shape the landscape during the Dreamtime.

Dreamtime Stories

Creation Stories

The Great Father

One day, Baiame, the great Ancestor Spirit, was walking through the land he had created, surveying all the plants and animals. Realizing something was missing, he made a man and a woman from dust and, setting them upright, told them that they might eat the plants but not the animals. In due course, the first man and woman had children and slowly but surely they began to populate the world. Everyone thanked Baiame and praised him for what he had done.

The Command is Broken

In time, the rain ceased to fall and the plants began to die. Horrified, more and more people fell sick with hunger. In desperation, one of the men broke Baiame's command and killed and ate a kangaroo rat, sharing it with his wife.

When the couple had eaten their fill, they offered some of the meat to a friend. Faint with hunger, the friend refused it and staggered away.

Death Enters the World

The man and woman decided to follow their friend's trail. At last, far in the distance, they spied him resting beneath a tree. As the couple stood there, they saw a black creature descend from the tree, snatch up their friend's body, and disappear back into the branches. Clutching each other in terror, they watched as the tree rose into the air and disappeared. And so it was that death entered the world.

The Wawilak Sisters

The story of the Wawilak sisters is the inspiration for an important cycle of ceremonies in north-east Arnhem Land. The story is re-enacted during the initiation ceremony of Yolngu boys.

The Journey

Long ago in the Dreamtime the two Wawilak sisters set off on a long journey through the land. As they walked, they sustained themselves with creatures and plants and gave names to everything they saw, bringing the landscape into existence. They began their travels somewhere in the interior and travelled northwards, towards Arnhem Land. One day, the two sisters met two men and lay with them, though to do so was taboo because it was incest as they were of the same moieties. Both women conceived and, in due course, the older of the sisters gave birth to a child. When the younger sister's time drew near, the women stopped by a waterhole and built a shelter in preparation for the birth.

The Rainbow Serpent is Disturbed

Unknown to the sisters, the mighty Rainbow Serpent lived in the pool. When the baby was born, blood from the birth seeped into the waterhole, polluting it and rousing the great snake. The creature rose high into the sky and, towering above the sisters, summoned up thunder, lightning and rain.

The Great Snake Strikes

Terrified, the sisters began to dance, hoping thereby to appease the monster. The Rainbow Serpent grew even angrier, however, so much so that the waterhole began to overflow causing a huge flood. At last the serpent bent down and swallowed the sisters in one gulp.

The Rainbow Serpent eventually regurgitated the sisters, who then instituted the initiation ceremonies of the Yolngu people of north-east Arnhem Land.

Djunban and the Flood

One day, say the Wirangu (or Wiranggu) people of South Australia, a man called Djunban was out hunting kangaroo rat with his magic boomerang when he struck his sister Mandjia by mistake, wounding her in the leg.

Djunban's Grief

Sometime later, Djunban taught his people how to make rain. Shortly afterwards, Mandjia died. When Djunban next performed the rain-making ceremony he was so grief stricken that he was unable to concentrate and the rain came down in torrents. Although he tried to warn his people, the waters rose and a great flood washed away all the people and their possessions. When the flood finally subsided all that was left was a hill of silt. The gold and bones that are found there come from those people of long ago.

The Rainbow Serpent's Tale

Long ago in the Dreamtime, the Rainbow Serpent emerged from beneath the ground and moved across the empty landscape, giving it form and shape. Some say that, after completing her travels, she went back to the place where she first emerged and called on the frogs to come out from underground. The frogs duly appeared, their bellies distended with water. When the Rainbow Serpent tickled them, they filled the tracks the great being had made with water, creating rivers and streams.

The Law of the Serpent

The Rainbow Serpent also introduced laws, as well as punishments for those who broke them. Many of the boulders scattered across Australia are said to be people whom the Rainbow Serpent turned to stone for ignoring her commands.

Lightning Man

Lightning Man or Namarrkon (or Namarrgon) is one of the great Ancestral Spirits of the Mayali people from Oenpelli in Arnhem Land. He carries axes with him at all times and throws them to the ground causing thunder and lightning. Namarrkon's two cousins constantly try to calm him down. Without their efforts, he would lash out at everyone he encounters. With luck, people are safe, but woe betide anyone carrying an axe.

Namarrkon Brings Rain

Some people say that Namarrkon is accompanied on his travels by his wife Barrginj and their children. The family entered the land from the north and brought with them rising sea levels, increased rainfall and tropical storms. At the rock-art site Nourlangie, Lightning Man is shown with stone axes attached to his head, elbows and knees.

The Seven Sisters

Long ago, before time began, the Sun sent two great Ancestral Spirits down to earth from the far end of the Milky Way.

These Ancestors made their way through the land, shaping the mountains and valleys, the lakes and the seas. When their work was almost done, the Sun sent down Seven Sisters – the Kungkarangalpe – from the Milky Way, instructing them to adorn the earth with flowers and trees, birds and beasts. So the Seven Sisters came down and began their work.

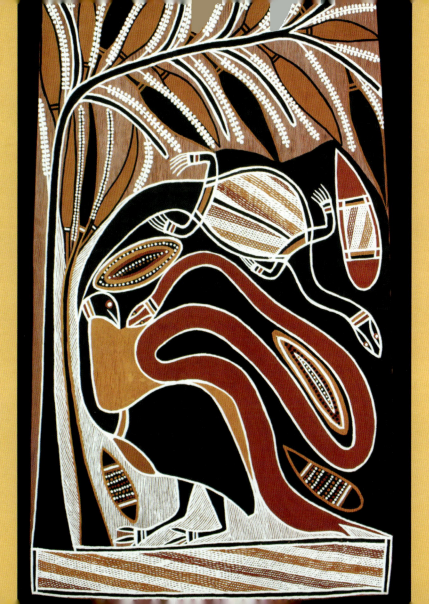

Drawn by Beauty

While the Seven Sisters were busy making the honey ants, they grew thirsty and so they sent the youngest of their number to find fresh water, pointing her towards the hills. All this time, the two Ancestral Spirits had been hiding in the bushes spying on the women. They crept quietly after the youngest sister, captivated by her beauty.

The Ancestors of the Desert People

When the Ancestors finally revealed themselves to the youngest sister, she thought they were very fine indeed and fell in love with them. The sun was outraged and forbade her to return to the stars. So the youngest sister and the two Ancestor beings remained on earth and it is they who are the ancestors of the desert people and gave them their laws.

Our story is in the land. It is written in those sacred places...

Bill Neidjie, *Gagadju Man*

Nyiru and the Seven Sisters

There was once an evil man called Nyiru who lusted after the Seven Sisters and planned to force himself on one of them. At this point in time, the sisters were travelling through the vast expanses of the Northern Territory.

The Sisters Set Up Camp

One night, the sisters stopped to camp, building a shelter which is now a low cliff. All the while Nyiru was watching them. In the morning the sisters moved on again. The place where they next set up camp is now a cave surrounded by fig trees; the tree standing alone is the oldest sister and the place where the sisters sat is marked by patterns in the rock.

A Near Escape

That night, Nyiru burst into the sisters' shelter, but they managed to escape through the back wall. The hole in the cave can be seen to this day.

The Sisters Become Stars

The sisters ran away as fast as they could until at last
they reached the coast and flung themselves into the sea. The
shock of the cold water made them leap high into the sky
where they remain to this day as the star cluster known in the
West as the Pleiades. Nyiru still chases them and can be seen
in the sky as the constellation Orion.

Animal Stories

The Namarrgan Sisters

The people of Ubirr in Kakadu National Park say that long ago, the two Namarrgan sisters were chatting by a billabong when one of them decided to take a stroll. When she reached the end of the billabong she suddenly thought it would be great fun to play a trick on her sister.

Tricks

Jumping into the water, the sister changed into a crocodile and swam back to where her sibling was sitting. When the massive crocodile leapt out, the sister was terrified. Delighted, the other sister played the same trick again and again. Finally, the duped sister realized what had been happening and so she decided to play the same game on her sister.

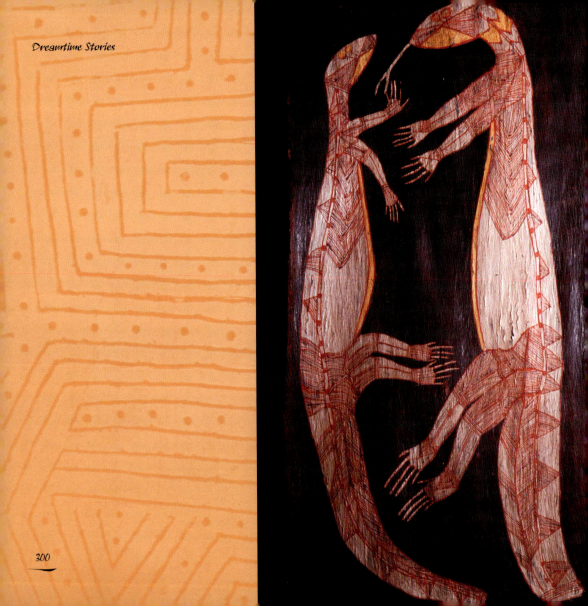

A Choice is Made

Day after day, the sisters played the same trick on each other until at last they both realized that if they changed permanently into crocodiles they would be able to eat anything and anybody they liked. Together, they made their way to the East Alligator River where they plunged into the water, and there they remain to this day.

Nintaka and Milbili

The Pitjantjatjara people of the Western Desert tell how, long ago, two lizards, one a perentie and the other a goanna, decided to decorate each other for a ceremony.

Nintaka the perentie was a talented artist and painted neat patterns of dots and lines all over the goanna's body and tail.

Slapdash Work

When it was time for Milbili the goanna to paint Nintaka, he took no trouble at all with his work. Instead, Milbili splashed the paint hither and thither without a care in the world. Nintaka asked how he looked whereupon Milbili assured him he was the handsomest creature ever to be seen.

Nintaka swaggered towards the ceremonial ground as pleased as can be. Unfortunately, however, he stopped to drink at a waterhole and there he saw his reflection shimmering up at him.

The Lizards are Separated

Nintaka rushed to attack Milbili but the goanna scurried to the top of a gum tree. Ever since then, the perentie and the goanna have lived in different habitats, and to this day the goanna's skin is delicately patterned whereas the perentie's skin is covered in random splodges.

The Jabiru and the Emu

The Marrkula people of Arnhem Land tell how, one day, Gandji and his children went fishing for stingray. The water was clear and they speared one fish after another with the greatest of ease. Afterwards, they took their catch back to camp where Gandji called his brother-in-law Wurrpan and his children to eat with them. However, Gandji kept all the best pieces of fish for his own family. When Wurrpan and his children realized what was happening, an argument broke out.

Gandji is Hurt

On and on the two men fought until finally Gandji threw hot coals at Wurrpan whereupon Wurrpan seized a rock and threw it at Gandji, hitting him in the chest. Gandji began to jump about in fear, bouncing higher and higher until at last he turned into a jabiru (stork) without a beak and flew away.

Gandji Gains a Beak

Grasping a spear, Wurrpan aimed it at the bird;
the weapon pierced through Gandji without harming him,
though its point protruded to form a beak.

Emus

Wurrpan and his children ran away and, as they did so, they began to change into emus.

The grey colour of emus' feathers is caused by the ashes from the hot coals, and their eggs are the same shape as the rock Wurrpan threw at Gandji.

The Crocodile and the Parrot

Once, long ago, shortly after fire had entered the world, a crocodile stole the only existing fire-stick and hurried off with it, heading for the Prince Regent River in north-west Kimberley. The other crocodiles were horrified, thinking fire would be extinguished for ever but, try as they might, they could not decide what to do. The great Ancestral Spirits also saw what was happening and sent a parrot to help out. While the crocodiles argued among themselves, the parrot flew down and escaped with the fire-stick under its wing.

Redwing

To this day the parrot is called a redwing and boasts a red patch of feathers as a reminder of the day he saved fire. The crocodile who stole the fire-stick was eventually speared in the guts whereupon his kidneys fell out. They can still be seen as red stones, lying scattered on the battleground.

319

Tumbi and Wodjin

A story from the Kimberly region of Australia tells how, one day, two boys were playing with an owl called Tumbi. They treated the poor bird shamefully, pulling his feathers, blinding him, then throwing him up into the air and laughing when he fell back down to earth. However, unbeknown to the two children, Tumbi was the son of an Ancestor or Wandjina Spirit called Inanunga, and the bird lost no time in complaining to his father.

Soon, all the Ancestors knew what had happened and, at the behest of an Ancestor called Wodjin, they agreed to punish the boys and their people.

Punishment

The Ancestors approached the people on a wide plain at Tunbai. Wodjin summoned up torrential rain by stroking his beard, while the birds danced on the wet ground, turning it to mud. Although the people fought back against the Ancestors, almost all of them soon perished in the mud. The two boys who had harmed the owl ran away, terrified, and sought shelter in a large boab tree. However, the tree was really an Ancestor and squeezed the boys to death. Tumbi the owl retired to a cave called Wanalirri near Gibb River. A rock-art image depicting Wodjin and his followers can still be seen there.

Stories of Death

The First Man to Die

The Worora people of the north-west Kimberley region of Western Australia say that long ago, Widjingara, one of the very first people, was killed by an Ancestor. Nobody knows quite why, since this all happened so far in the past. Widjingara was the first human being ever to die. His wife was terribly shocked and had no idea what to do. In her bewilderment, she shaved her head and coated herself with ashes.

A Second Death

As it turned out, this first death had not been carried out in quite the right way and three days later Widjingara came back to life. The poor man was so terrified at the sight of his wife in her shaved and ashen state that he died all over again.

327

The Djuan Elder

According to the Djuan people of Queensland, there was once a wise man, an Elder, who had done more than anyone else to help them. He had taught them how to hunt and how to resolve disputes and how to live peacefully together; he had taught them how to enjoy the fruits of nature and how to share their food.

A Song to Remember

When the Elder realized his time was coming to an end, he travelled from camp to camp, stopping at each one to sing a song. This song would be passed down through the generations, reassuring the Djuan people that the Elder was still looking after them.

Soon after he sang to his people, the Elder died, and now the Djuan believe that the Milky Way is the smoke from his heavenly camp fire.

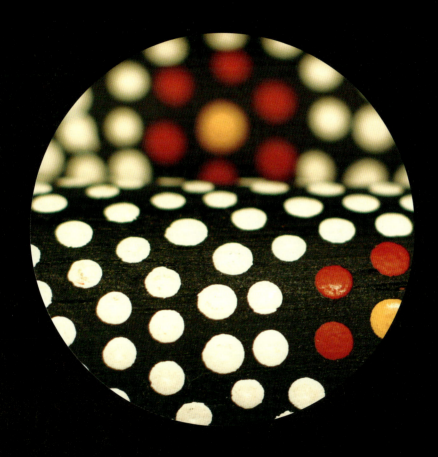

Tiwi Death Myth

Long ago, in the Dreamtime, everyone was happy and death had not yet entered the world. In those days, there was a man called Purukupali (or Purrukurpali) who went hunting one morning, leaving his wife Wai-ai (or Pima) to gather food. The moment Purukupali was out of sight, Wai-ai hurried into the bush, some say to play with her friends, others say to meet with her lover, Thapara. Wai-ai scarcely spared a thought for her baby whom she had left behind at the camp, all alone. That day the sun beat down so strongly and there was so little shade that the baby died.

Death Becomes Part of Life

When Purukupali found out what had happened to his child he was furious. Thapara said he could bring the baby back to life in three days but Purukupali would not listen to him. Taking his dead son in his arms he walked backwards into the sea saying that from now on everyone would experience death.

Stories of Everyday Life

The Didjeridu

Aborigines from the Northern Territory say that there was once a hunter, named Yidaki, who was returning home with his catch one day when he saw a dead branch lying on the ground. Picking it up, he noticed it was filled with insects and tried to blow them out. The sound the hunter made was so beautiful that he took the branch home and played it to his people. From that time onwards, they used the didjeridu in many of their ceremonies.

When Yidaki died, his spirit entered the didjeridu. To this day, if you hold the instrument to your ear and listen carefully, you can sometimes hear him playing it.

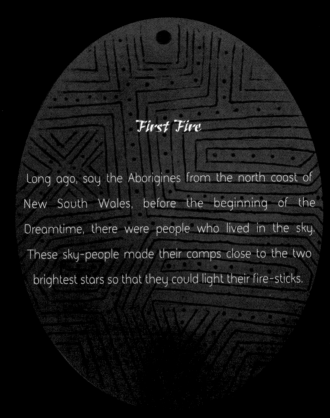

First Fire

Long ago, say the Aborigines from the north coast of New South Wales, before the beginning of the Dreamtime, there were people who lived in the sky. These sky-people made their camps close to the two brightest stars so that they could light their fire-sticks.

Descent to Earth

Day followed day, the food began to run out and life in the sky-world grew harsh. At last, two brave brothers, Kanbi and Jitabi, decided to venture down to earth to collect nuts and berries and hunt possums. They promised to bring back plentiful supplies of food for everyone. So the brothers descended to earth and, leaving their fire-sticks smouldering at their camp, they set off on a hunt. The hunt dragged on and the fire-sticks grew bored and began to play games. They ran from place to place and everywhere they went, they set light to the grass until there was a huge blaze.

Fire on Earth

Seeing the smoke, the two brothers hurried back to their camp. The people who lived in the region saw the smoke too and gathered to marvel at the extraordinary sight, for they had never seen fire before. Some of the brothers' catch was lying near the flames and began to cook. The people's mouths watered at the delicious smell. Fearing that the earth people would be angry with them for causing such a disturbance, the brothers rushed back to the sky. By now, however, the people had lit their own fire-sticks and were delighted that from this time onwards they would be able to cook their food.

The Dolphin Wife

The Wanungamulangwa people of Groote Island say that at the very beginning of time, an Ancestor Spirit called Dinginjabana lived as a dolphin in the waters around their home. Dinginjabana was a brave and strong dolphin but his wife, Ganadja, was quiet and fearful. Dinginjabana liked to tease the yakuna shellfish for being stuck fast to the coral. Although Ganadja begged him to be kinder, Dinginjabana would not listen. The yakuna, on the other hand, mocked the dolphins for their mindless chatter and none was more scathing than Baringgwa.

Dinginjabana is a Bully

One day, Dinginjabana prised Baringgwa from the coral and tossed him through the air to his friends. Baringgwa begged for mercy but the dolphins would not listen. All of a sudden Baringgwa shouted out in terror that the tiger sharks, who were enemies of the dolphins, were coming. Still the dolphins would not listen. And so the sharks attacked the dolphins and many of them, including Dinginjabana, were slaughtered. Ganadja was safe, sheltered by the yakunas, but she was grief-stricken at the loss of her husband. The yakunas tried to comfort her, saying that Dinginjabana had become one of the two-legged creatures that walk on earth, but Ganadja remained distraught.

Ganadja Becomes Human

One night, Ganadja swam close to shore and managed to pull herself to land, laboriously working her way up the sand. At long last, she was transformed into a woman and set off on foot to find her husband.

The Thukeri Fish

The Ngarrindjerri people of the lower River Murray area of South Australia say that there were once two men who set off fishing together in their canoe. Having found a good spot, they stopped and lowered their lines. All day long the two men pulled up the most plump and delicious Thukeri fish. By the end of the day their canoe was almost overflowing.

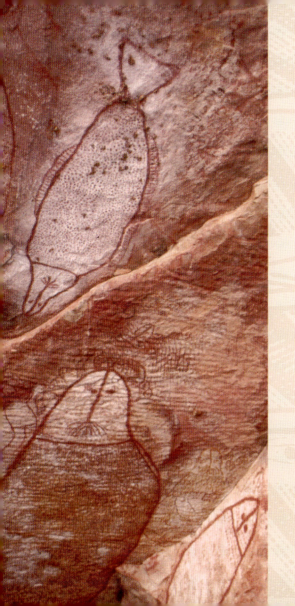

A Lie

As the men paddled delightedly to shore they saw a stranger who appeared to be walking straight towards them. Panicking in case he should want to share their catch with them, the men quickly hid the fish. The moment they landed, the stranger begged the fishermen for a fish or two, saying he had eaten nothing all day. The two men claimed they had caught only one or two fish and that they needed those to feed their families. The stranger turned away, but as he did so he said that the fishermen had lied and that they would therefore never again enjoy a Thukeri fish.

A Valuable Lesson

The fishermen thought nothing of what had happened – until, that is, they began to gut the fish. Those beautiful, plump creatures were now nothing but bones and impossible to eat.

When the men returned home, the Elders told them that the stranger must have been the great Ancestor Spirit Ngurunderi. And so it was that Ngurunderi taught the Ngarrindjeri people a lesson they would long remember.

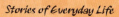

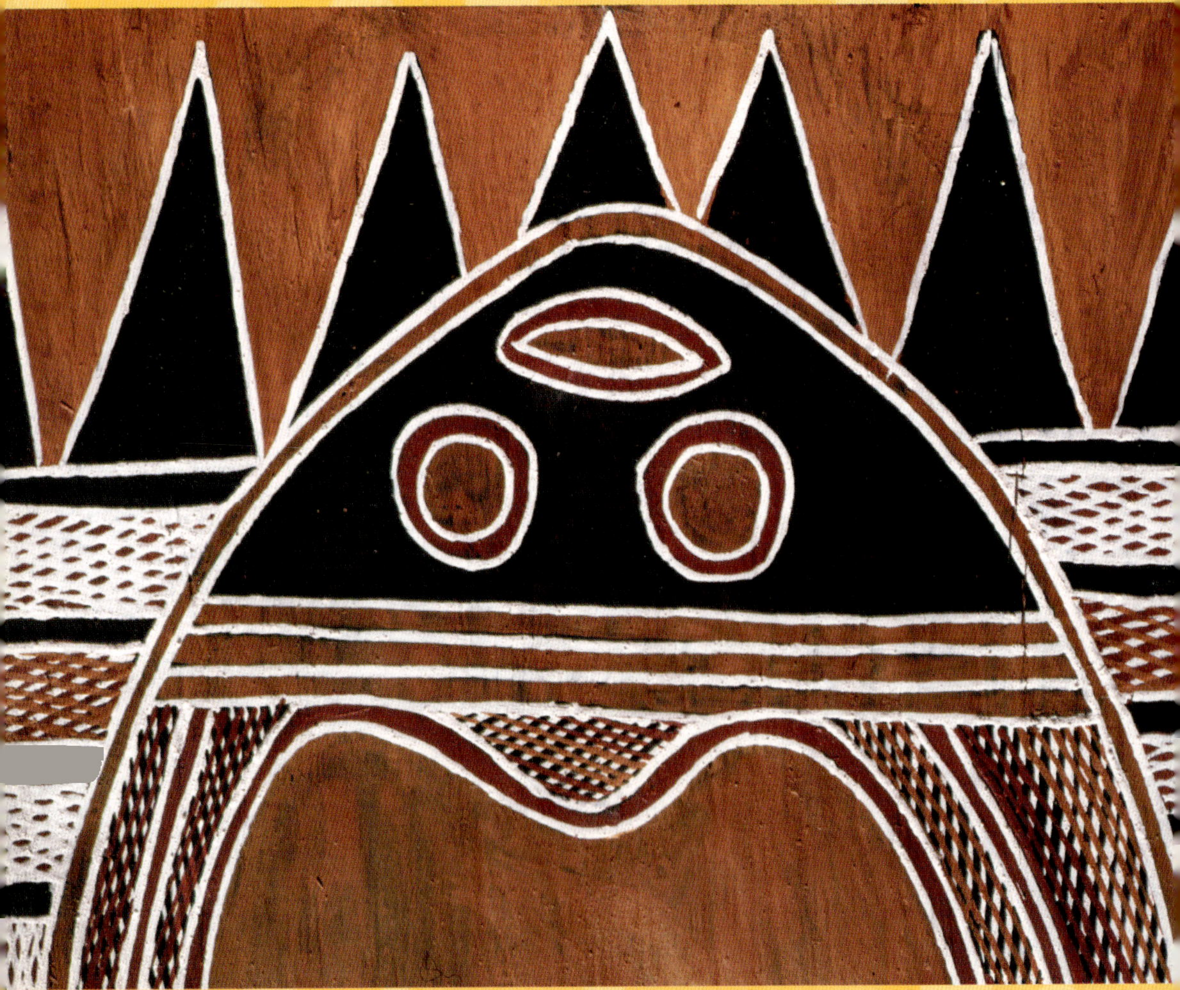

Totyerguil and Otchout

According to the Wotojobaluk people of Victoria, there was once a hunter called Totyerguil who was camping near Swan Hill when his two sons found a massive fish called Otchout in a nearby waterhole.

A Chase Begins

The boys ran to tell their father of their discovery whereupon Totyerguil paddled out to the fish, and threw his spear at it. The spear lodged in the fish's back and stayed there, sticking upwards. Attempting to escape, Otchout swam furiously to the edge of the waterhole and began to tear through the ground creating a channel. Indeed, the fish moved so quickly that Totyerguil could scarcely keep up with it.

Totyerguil Persists

That evening, Otchout made a huge billabong and rested there for the night. However, Totyerguil had not given up and threw another spear at the monster. This spear also stayed sticking up out of the fish's back. And so it went on for several days, the fish creating a vast channel by burrowing through the land with Totyerguil following in hot pursuit, throwing one spear after another at the creature. Eventually Totyerguil had no spears left and so, reluctantly, he gave up the chase. These spears are now the spines that can be seen sticking out of the back of the codfish. The channel Otchout created became the Murray River.

Stories of the Landscape

How Uluru was Formed

Long ago, the Mala people travelled across the land until they came to the place where Uluru now stands. They stopped there and set up camp, the young and old at separate sites as well as the men and women. The Elders planted a ceremonial pole in the ground and, close to Kantju waterhole, they all began preparations for a great ceremony.

Boys Play

Two boys out hunting heard the sound of the preparations and, curious, hurried towards the source of the noise. When they reached the waterhole there was nobody there since all the Mala people were busy collecting food. Bored, the boys sat down and began to play, mixing water with sand and earth and piling it up higher and higher.

Mount Conner

Eventually, to their surprise, the boys found they had created the huge mound now called Uluru. They began to slide down their huge mud pile, dragging their fingers through the mud as they did so. The long channels they formed can still be seen on the south side of Uluru. The Mala, meanwhile, had been attacked by Kurpany, a giant black dog, and had fled. The boys, however, were safe and they made their way to the summit of Mount Conner, about 88 km (50 miles) south-east of Uluru, where they can still be seen in the form of boulders.

The Kuniya People

A long time ago a group of Python Ancestors known as the Kuniya people approached Uluru from three different directions. One of the women carried eggs on her head and buried them to the east of Uluru and one of them sat down on the summit of the rock, leaving depressions in its surface. Gradually, they all settled into a peaceful way of life at Uluru: the women gathered fruit and seeds while the men hunted.

Attack

One day, the Kuniya people were attacked by the poisonous snake men known as the Liru. The marks left by the warriors' spears can still be seen on the south-west face of Uluru. At Mutitjulu Gorge the Liru leader, Kulikudgeri, and a young Kuniya man fought each other singlehanded. The gashes they made with their stone knives can still be seen on the west face of the gorge. Eventually, the Kuniya man was so badly wounded that he staggered away to die. The water that flows into the gorge records the path he took and three pools high on the rock mark where he stopped to rest.

Gelam and Usar

Long ago, a young boy named Gelam lived with Usar, his
mother, on the island of Moa (Banks Island) in the Torres Strait.
One day, Usar gave him a bow and arrow and sent him off
to hunt pigeons. Being greedy, Gelam saved all the fat pigeons
for himself and gave his mother the birds that were only
skin and bone. Usar soon discovered here son's greed
and devised a plan.

Usar Surprises Gelam

Covering herself in clay, Usar hid by the path where Gelam went hunting. The moment Gelam came close, she jumped out. Terrified, Gelam ran back to the camp but his mother beat him to it. By the time Gelam arrived, Usar was sitting comfortably beside the fire. Usar played the same trick on Gelam day after day until finally he realized what was happening.

Gelam Leaves

The next day Gelam left home. His mother stood on a reef gazing after him and weeping copiously. First of all Gelam swam to Yam Island, then to York Island and then to Darnley Island. Wherever he went, he could still see his mother standing on the reef, weeping. Then Gelam swam out to a little island east of Darnley and from there he could no longer see his mother.

The Islands are Created

Gelam lay down and sneezed out two seeds which formed the islands of Dauar and Waier. Then a stingray sheltered close to him and formed the island of Mer (Murray Island). Usar stayed standing on the reef weeping until the tide came in and covered her. She remains there still as a rock; at low tide her tears can be seen flowing from a hole in the centre of the stone.

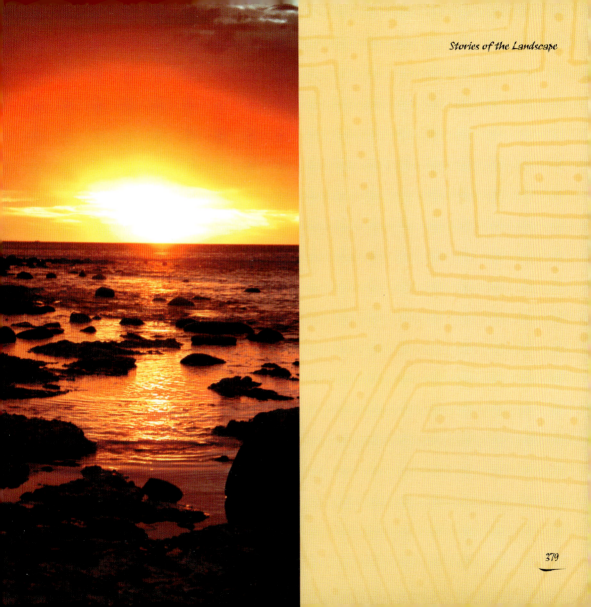

Further Reading

Berndt, Ronald M. and Berndt, Catherine *The Speaking Land: Myth and Story in Aboriginal Australia*

(Penguin, Melbourne, 1989)

Ellis, Jean A. *From the Dreamtime: Australian Aboriginal Legends* (Collins Dove, Victoria, 1991)

Flood, Josephine *Archaeology of the Dreamtime: The Story of Prehistoric Australia and its People*

(Yale University Press, New Haven, 1990)

Gilbert, K. (ed) *Inside Black Australia: an Anthology of Aboriginal Poetry* (Penguin Books, Ringwood, 1988)

Isaacs, Jennifer *Australian Dreaming: 40,000 years of Aboriginal History* (Lansdowne Press, Sydney, 1980)

Kleinert, Sylvia and Neale, Margo (eds) *The Oxford Companion to Aboriginal Art and Culture*

(Oxford University Press, Melbourne, 2000)

Lawlor, Robert *Voices of the First Day: Awakening in the Aboriginal Dreamtime* (Inner Traditions, Rochester, 1991)

Neidjie, B. *Gagadju Man* (JB Books, Marleston, 2002)

Reed, A.W. *Aboriginal Myths, Legends & Fables* (Reed Books, Sydney, 1982)

Rose, Deborah *Nourishing Terrains: Australian Aboriginal Views of Landscape and Wilderness*

(Australian Heritage Commission, Canberra, 1996)

Stanner, W.H.E. *White Man Got No Dreaming, Essays 1938–1973* (ANUP, Canberra, 1979)

Tonkinson, Robert *The Mardudjara Aborigines: Living the Dream in Australia's Desert*

(Holt, Rinehart and Wilson, New York, 1978)

Websites

Stories of the Dreaming: www.dreamtime.net.au/dreaming

Kakadu National Park: www.environment.gov.au/parks/kakadu/

Aboriginal Art Online: www.aboriginalartonline.com

Picture Credits

All pictures courtesy of the following picture agencies and artists, and the creative manipulation of Lucy Robins.

Corbis: 8 & 120–21 & 266–67, 28–29, 36 & 324, 40–41, 44–45 & 142–43 & 308–09, 46–47 & 179 & 358–59 (David Malangi), 48–49, 54–55, 56, 60–61 & 220–21, 63, 64–65 & 112 & 351, 68–69 (Clifford Possum), 74 & 336–37, 88–89 & 182–83, 90 & 190–91 & 376–77, 96–97 & 214–15 (Two Bob), 98, 102–03, 110–11 & 244–45, 118–19 & 232, 122–23 & 251, 126–27, 128–29, 130–31 & 212–13, 139 & 254–255 (Dhartangu), 140, 144, 146–47 & 224–25, 148–49, 150–51, 152–53, 156–57 (Sammy Butcher), 165, 168–69 & 269, 176–77 & 264–65 (George Milpurrurru), 186–87 & 372–73 (Dhartangu), 188–89, 203 & 355 (Banapana), 211 (Binyinuwuy), 229 (Terry Yumbulul), 234–35 & 328 (David Malangi), 236–37 & 310–11 (Terry Yumbulul), 242–43, 261, 278–79, 280–81 (David Malangi), 285, 300, 316–17, 319, 326–27, 338–39 & 374–75, 342–43, 344–45, 356–57

Shutterstock: 4–7 & 303, 14–15, 16–17 & 162–63, 19 & 108–09, 20–21 & 172 & 277, 23 & 286–87, 24, 26–27, 31 & 158–59, 32–33 & 304–05, 34–35 & 288–89, 38–39, 43, 50–51, 52–53, 59, 67 & 104–05, 70–71, 72–73, 77 & 134–35, 78–79, 81 & 294, 82–83 & 258–59, 84–85, 92–93, 94–95, 101, 106–07, 115, 116, 124–25, 136–37, 154–55, 158–59, 166–67, 170, 174–75, 180–81, 184–85, 192 & 340, 195, 196, 198–99, 200–01, 204–05, 206–07, 208, 219, 223, 226–27, 230, 239, 240–41, 247, 248–49, 262, 270–71, 272–73, 274, 282–83, 290–291, 293, 296–97, 299, 306–07, 313, 315, 320, 323, 332–33, 335, 346–47, 348–49, 360–61, 362–63, 364, 366–67, 368, 370–71, 379

iStockphoto: 86–87 & 352, 216–17, 256–57

Fotolia: 161 & 331

Index